EXILE
REVISITED

Also by James B. Johnston

The Price of Peace
www.priceofpeace.net

EXILE
REVISITED

James B. Johnston

Celtic Cat Publishing
KNOXVILLE, TENNESSEE

Revised editon. The first edition was published by Celtic Cat
Publishing in 1997 under the title *Exile: Poems of an Irish
Immigrant* (0-9658950-0-9)

Celtic Cat Publishing
2654 Wild Fern Lane
Knoxville, Tennessee 37931
www.celticcatpublishing.com

Manufactured in the United States of America
Design by Dariel Mayer
Cover photograph by Jim Johnston

ISBN: 978-0-9847836-1-8

Library of Congress Control Number: 2011963538

For Ann,
Whose love bridges our differences,
and for my children,
Réjean, Marie, and Deirdre Lynne.

CONTENTS

SECTION II

The Land of My Exile

Exile Revisited

"Memory of the past is a prize worth struggling for."
—Tina Rosenberg, *The Haunted Land*

I published *Exile* in 1997 to gain first-hand knowledge about publishing. Since then, I've published nineteen books written by other authors. *Exile* is no longer in print, so the time feels right to issue a revised and expanded edition. The primary changes are the addition of essays and a few new poems.

Like many before us, Ann and I didn't want to leave Northern Ireland. We had strong bonds with our families. We had good jobs. We had lots of friends. But there was a smoking gun—the increasing and sectarian nature of violence in the early 1970s and the related threat to our planned marriage.

Although we both grew up in Belfast, within a few miles of each other, I was brought up a Protestant in the British tradition while Ann was brought up a Catholic in the Irish tradition. For the most part, this was not a factor in our daily lives. However, as the Troubles escalated in 1970 and the violence moved from stone throwing to burning houses and then to sectarian killings, the two communities quickly polarized and fear entered our lives. In spite of the arrival of British troops, the growth of multiple paramilitary organizations raised violence to new levels.

In 1972 and 1973, there were in excess of 15,000 shootings, 3,000 bombings and 700 deaths. To put this in perspective, Ireland is about three-quarters the size of Tennessee. Northern Ireland, where we lived and where most of the violence occurred, is about one-eighth the size of Tennessee. Most of the dead, including some of our friends, were innocent civilians, in the wrong place at the wrong time.

In the broadest sense, exile has more to do with an involuntary state of mind than with one's physical happenstance. We can be exiles in our own land. Exile touches on the deepest emotions experienced by those who are separated, for whatever reason, from the people, places or things they love the most. In its early stages, it is characterized by a deep hunger for the past, a longing that, at times, is almost too much to bear. In such a context, exile places a premium on memory. How much we cling to memory was brought home to me in a vivid way in 1976.

Mary McIlwain was born in Ireland in April 1893. She immigrated to Canada in 1910 and died four years later from tuberculosis. In the summer of 1976, my mother, then a sprightly seventy-two, visited Canada for the first time. When asked if there was anything special that she wanted to do, she brought out an old photograph of a headstone. On the back of the photograph were the words "Newmarket, Ontario."

Armed with this scant but valuable information, we began a successful search for the grave of her sister, Mary. When my mother placed fresh flowers on that grave, I knew that it would not matter what else she would do during the remainder of her visit. It would be a memorable holiday. My mother had brought to closure an exile she had endured silently from that day when, as a six-year-old, she had clung to her mother's skirts as Mary said good-bye.

When I look at the old photograph, I think of the compassion the photographer had for a grieving family thousands of miles away. I think of the importance of taking the time to preserve our memories. The photographer did not know my mother would visit Canada. Memories are a lifeline between a definitive past and an uncertain future.

Like a photographer, my poems and essays try to capture a precise moment in time—sometimes an event, other times an emotion. Sometimes they capture joy, other times pain. But always they are preserving the past and the present for the future.

Ironically, it was my own exile that provided the impetus for my mother to visit Canada and the opportunity for her to visit Mary's grave. For Ann and myself, this exile, which began with great sadness, was a turning point in our lives. It marked the beginning of our life together.

We have lived longer in North America than we did in Ireland. We have experienced living in such diverse places as metropolitan Toronto, a city of three million people; Terrace Bay, a small community of 2500 on the north shore of Lake Superior; Sylacauga, in hot and humid Alabama, and Knoxville, Tennessee, set in the foothills of the beautiful Smoky Mountains.

On this journey, we have had the enriching and challenging experience of adopting three children. We have been fortunate that most years we have had the opportunity to go back to Ireland. We go to places we have not visited before. We see familiar sites through new eyes. It is a measure of how small the world really is that when we are in Tennessee, we call Ireland home, and when we are in Ireland, we call Tennessee home.

In April 1997, while visiting Ireland, I was shown a copy of the death notice inserted by "Aunt Martha" in a Canadian newspaper at the time of Mary's death. It contained a wealth of information, naming her parents, the three pallbearers and the minister who conducted the service at her Canadian home and grave. The obituary concluded with this simple but poignant poem:

In a far and distant graveyard,
Where the trees their branches wave,
Lies a loving niece and daughter,
In a cold and silent grave.

As with the first edition, *Exile Revisited* is very much about preserving the past—people and places, family, friends and strangers, the living and the dead, experiences good and not so good. Like Mary, may they not be forgotten.

—JAMES B. JOHNSTON
May 2012

SECTION I

The Land of My Birth

Exile

When advancing years slow my steps
And my mind turns increasingly
To the contemplation of past years,
Will I, in exile, fondly remember
The land of my birth? The land
I left when fear shrouded
The serenity of family life;
When bullets and bombs
Overshadowed the beauty of the mountains
And the music of the streams, and
My search for true freedom found fulfillment
In a new life in a strange land.

Will my recollections be of seashore walks
And Sunday outings, terraced houses
With their open-hearth warmth,
The milkman and his empties,
The pub and draft beer,
The charcoal-coated chimney sweep,
Brushes atop his shoulder?
Or will I only recall
Bricked up houses and barbed-wire police stations,
Soldiers and searches, road ramps and rioting,
The deaths and division that made me leave
The island that was my home, the island
That is my home?

Holy Ground

Flight fatigue fades fast
As the first green fields
Filter their welcome through
Rain-filled clouds.
I raise myself up,
Craning to catch sight
Of Belfast Lough,
Napoleon's Nose or
The giant Goliath cranes
That wait expectantly
For another Titanic.
As the twin prop banks steeply,
Fields and hedgerows,
Knit together like some
Patterned patchwork quilt,
Rise up to meet me.

Unquiet Grave

Flowers,
Wild upon a grave.
In memoriam.

Words on stone,
Worn by weather.
Speaking of life,
Birth, death,
Love, sorrow.

Sleeping the last sleep.

Anna L. Johnston, 1904–1995

Origins

I go back to the place of my birth,
To the one who conceived me.
As the casket is opened, one last time,
I look on the face of infinite love,
I experience the pain of parting.
I know you are ready to go.
You told me so, four years ago,
When pain first marked the fragility of time,
And, with words crafted on labored breath,
You longed for the breath of God
To push away the clouds
And reveal the Son.

I wish I had spent more time with you,
Building memories, capturing and cultivating
Your gentleness and strength;
The tolerance that built bridges,
The warmth that made our friends your friends,
The courage to let your children grow,
The simplicity of your faith.
It is too late to talk about how you met Dad,
Having children in your forties,
Your successful business venture,
So I close the casket. The sun has set.
There are no clouds.

The Garden

It is a season
Of contentment.
With spade and rake
Mother and daughter
Built this Eden
Stone by stone,
Weeding, planting,
Pruning, transplanting.
One caring for the garden,
The other for the gardener.

Oh sister,
The rose-covered
Trellis is no more.
It is now the season
Of grief.
You wear it as a cloak,
It has become life itself.
You look out at Gethsemane
With sorrow's sightless stare
And see a wilderness of weeds,
Emptiness filled with melancholy.

Oh sister,
This season too will pass.
When you see the snowdrop,
Healing begins.

The Artisan

On the cover of my school books
You would paint a sunset,
On a disk of discarded wood
You would paint a sea,
In my mind's eye
You have painted yourself.

Richard Johnston. 1877–1963

Gentle Man

Many years have passed now,
But still I remember how
At eighty-three
You would walk to work,
Gait straight,
Taking your time,
Occasionally
Pausing
To catch breath,
Or in that way
So characteristic of your age,
To touch your hat
In formal recognition of a friend.

Rocky Road

Set at the foot of
The Castlereagh hills,
The steep winding Rocky Road
Was the site of our Sunday ramble.
It was not a time for gadding about,
Nor for that matter for dilly-dallying.
Single file was the dictate of the day,
And on occasions when we broke formation,
My father would tap us with his blackthorn walking stick
And, much to our amusement, remind us that we were not
Brown's cows.

Fencing Frontiers

Before I built a wall I'd ask to know
What I was walling in or walling out.
— Robert Frost

It seems to me that we live in a world where the response to fear is increasingly to build walls that provide protection. These walls, or fences, are commonly referred to as segregation barriers.

Sometimes they are designed to prevent illegal immigration or the smuggling of illegal drugs. However, for the most part, they are built to keep two populations apart and are anti-terror or anti-immigration in nature.

I was born on an island of stone wall fences. In spite of the island being only 250 miles wide and 350 miles long, it is estimated that Ireland has over 250,000 miles of stone walls. Ireland is naturally stony so clearing the land of stones allows the land to be farmed. The stones then can be used to build fences, to mark land divisions. Most of the walls are built without tools. They are dry stone walls. No mortar holds the stones together. The art is in selecting boulders that will balance, one upon the other. Some of these fences clearly do not serve the purpose of defining boundaries. They run from the bottom of a mountain to the top of the mountain. These are the famine walls built to provide employment during the Great Famines of the nineteenth century. Whatever the reason for their existence, these stone fences are objects of great beauty.

Until I was twenty-nine, I lived in a city of fences. These fences did not exist at the time of my birth. The first fences were built in the early 1970s, following the outbreak of "The Troubles." Belfast now has over twenty Peace Lines. While they mark battle lines, they also serve to minimize intercommunal strife between Protestants and Catholics. The Peace Lines range in length from a few hundred yards to

Stone walls in the Mourne Mountains

over three miles. The most prominent barriers are in West Belfast where they separate the predominantly Catholic Falls Road from the Protestant Shankill Road and in East Belfast where they separate the mainly Catholic Short Strand from the mainly Protestant Cluan Place. The Peace Lines are up to twenty-five feet high, constructed of corrugated steel and topped with barbed wire. While the Peace Lines are not objects of beauty, they provide something beautiful—peace of mind to the fearful residents who shelter behind them. It is unlikely these walls will come down anytime soon.

Of course, fences and separation barriers are not unique to Ireland. In the third century B.C. a series of stone and earthen barriers, known today as the Great Wall of China, were constructed to separate the Empire of China from Mongolia and Manchuria. There are approximately 1,500 miles of fortifications and the wall averages twenty-five feet in height.

Perhaps the most famous separation barrier in modern times is the Berlin Wall, a 96 mile concrete and barbed wire barrier built in 1961 to separate West Berlin from East Berlin and the rest of East Germany. Unlike most fences which are built to keep people out, the Berlin Wall, much like a prison wall, was constructed to keep people in. The wall was torn down in 1989 with the collapse of communism and the ending of the Cold War. Ironically, the 40 year old Belfast barriers have outlived the Berlin Wall which came down after twenty-eight years.

In more recent times, in response to suicide bombings and terror attacks against Israelis, the Israeli government, under pressure from its citizens, began the construction of the Israeli West Bank fence, a barrier that separates the Israeli and Palestinian populations. Most of the barrier is a multi-layered barbed wire fence system that includes anti-vehicle ditches and intrusion detection equipment. High concrete walls form approximately ten percent of the barrier. More than 300 miles of the fence have been completed and, upon completion, the fence may stretch for 500 miles.

Closer to home, the United States has built its own fences along parts of the border with Mexico to combat the

Peace Line in West Belfast

movement of illegal drugs and illegal immigrants into the United States. As the debate on illegal immigration intensifies, there is significant discussion on a proposal to build a further 700 miles of fencing along parts of the border.

In his poem *Mending Wall,* Robert Frost suggests that the wall that separates his property from his neighbor's property is unnecessary:

> "He is all pine and I am apple orchard.
> My apple trees will never get across
> And eat the cones under his pines...."

However, his neighbor simply reiterates what his father had taught him:

> "Good fences make good neighbors."

As the frontiers of earth become more accessible, it appears that Frost's neighbor may be right. There seems to be an increased desire among many communities to live apart from their neighbors. Since 2000, separation barriers have been constructed in Spain, Turkmenistan, Uzbekistan, Afghanistan, Botswana, Zimbabwe, India, Saudi Arabia, Yemen, Brunei, Egypt, China, North Korea, Kazakhstan, and Italy. Separation barriers are under construction in Iraq, Iran, United Arab Emirates, Oman, United States and Israel. Other fences have been proposed in Thailand, Malaysia, Pakistan and Chechnya. Almost all of these are anti-terror, anti-immigration, anti-drug smuggling measures or result from local or regional conflicts.

Robert Frost recognized that the construction of fences sometimes makes sense. For example, ranchers who own cattle or horses logically erect fences to keep their animals from trespassing on their neighbor's property. We fence in swimming pools for the safety of small children. It may be that fencing our frontiers is a valid response to conflict, terrorism, illegal immigration and smuggling. However, Frost's doubt that fences automatically make for good neighbors acknowledges the downside of building fences, particularly

17

over the longer term — segregation results not only in social exclusion but fortifies and breeds sectarianism.

In Northern Ireland there is peace on paper and, for now, on the streets. However, as long as the two communities in Northern Ireland live within separate enclaves, sectarianism will remain, making that peace fragile. This is true not just in Northern Ireland but throughout the world. Sadly, there is no short-term fix. The reality is that fences will come down only when there is a genuine peace within the hearts of people. For this to happen, the fears that fueled the construction of fences in the first place must be eliminated. Fears built up over years of conflict and violence take years to dissipate. Perhaps part of a line from the poem "Lake Isle of Innisfree" by William Butler Yeats best captures this truth:

"For peace comes dropping slow,"

Stone Wall Fences

Rising a modest twenty-eight hundred feet above the sea,
The Mountains of Mourne are all mountains to me.
How often their steep granite slopes have drawn me
From the confines of the city. How often, as children,
We followed the river Glen through Donard Forest.
Little we knew of oak and beech, elm and sycamore.
Our goal, to reach the open hillside, cross the stile and
Recapture our breath at the old icehouse on Thomas Mountain.

Today, again, we have left Belfast for the tranquility of the Mournes,
A Belfast bracing for bombs even as it gathers for peace.
Later, at three, we too will gather in the foothills of these mountains
To pursue the pollen of peace. This morning Slieve Donard
Is capped with a dusting of snow, but a welcome sun takes
The chill off a cold February morning as we rest alongside
The Mourne wall. I recall seeing an old stonemason maintain this wall.
He set stone upon stone with roughened hands,
Building with care this wall of beauty and strength.

We are a land divided by stone wall fences and granite hearts.

We go on to the Silent Valley to experience, for a moment,
Complete stillness. This valley is an ocean apart from the bombs
That marked the cease-fire cessation. We want to tarry longer, but
Three o'clock approaches—as if our silent scream will be decisive
In restoring the cease-fire—two of ten thousand souls trying to
Make everything like it was just so, dismantling the walls of
Granite hearts, peace by piece.

Ann Owens, 1949–1972

Ann

We first met when we went to Rathmore,
The Convent of the Sacred Heart of Mary.
Our birthdays, seven days apart.
How you enjoyed your week of seniority!
Do you remember our trips to the Gaeltacht and Scotland,
My refusal to wear glasses at Saturday night dances,
How you would tell me who was cute and who was who?
It was not what we did that mattered, but doing it together.
You were my best friend,
Kind and dreamy,
Quiet, with a soft-spoken sense of humor.
We understood time. Eight meant nine.
All of life was before us.

I look at my last photograph of you,
Sitting on a cannon at Edinburgh Castle.
How soon weapons of war would steal away our time.
When I visited in hospital after the first bombing,
You smiled and said, *I've had my turn.*
I wish it was true.
How little we knew.

I think often of that Saturday, seven months later.
You phoned mid-morning and asked me to meet you in town.
I couldn't go, but you promised to visit on your way home.
I remember the first phone call, late afternoon, asking if
I'd heard about the bomb.
I brushed it off. I knew you weren't near it.
When your parents phoned to say you hadn't arrived home,
I told them not to worry, traffic had been disrupted.
But I was worried.
It was unlike you not to phone.
By bedtime I was in a panic.
I asked my dad to call your parents one last time.
When he said *Oh Jesus*
I knew you would never phone.

Farringdon Gardens, in the Ardoyne district of Belfast

Farringdon Gardens

The fires have died a death,
Only their ghosts remain
In the buildings' somber shells,
Where people once
Lived, laughed, loved,
Worried, cried, died,
Hoped hopes that too have died
In the ruins of this charred community,
Forced by fear
To fire their homes
And flee.

A memorial to the victims of the
Kingsmills massacre

Last Ride

At Kingsmills Cross
On the Whitecross-Newry road,
A waving red light
Penetrates the dusk,
Signals the minibus to stop.

The casual chatter
Of workers returning home
From the Glenanne textile factory
Fades to a steely silence
As the bus slows, then stops.

The door opens.
A masked gunman enters,
Barks a command.
Filled with fear
The workers file
Out into the
Darkness.

Eleven more gunmen.

The passengers line up
Along the roadside,
State their religion.
A sole Roman Catholic
Is hustled away.
Ten Protestants stand
Together.

Machine gun fire.

For ten,
One last ride
In South Armagh.

Lonely Farm

The harvest has long since passed.
Christmas has come and gone,
Bringing a New Year
With all its promises
Of peace and prosperity.

The January dusk falls early.
At the end of a long lane,
Two miles from Gilford,
Darkness surrounds
A secluded farmhouse.

Inside,
Crowded relatives celebrate reunion.
Barry plays piano.
Tomorrow he will return
To an oil rig in the Orkney Islands.

Outside,
Wearing diamond mesh masks,
Carrying automatic weapons,
Guided by light from within,
Three strangers approach.

They knock on the door.
A relative answers.
In vain she tries
To slam it
Shut.

The strangers rush past her,
Firing at point-blank range.
Barry, brother Declan,
Uncle Joseph fall dying
On top of four young children.

Tonight in Ballydoogan,
The promise of peace
Perishes on a lonely farm
In Ireland.

The Grim Reaper

Death's cold grip descended on Dominic with
A last panic-stricken cry, "Jesus, help me Mary,"
    Swift and violent as his terrorist past.
    Witnessed by his teenaged son,
    The renegade Republican was
    Pulled from a public call box,
        Shot ten times.
        Right knee,
        Left knee,
        Stomach,
        Chest,
        Neck,
        Head,
        Dead.

Louvain, Belgium 1971

On this twelfth day of July,
Seeking shelter from the sun,
I walk along the narrow lanes
Of gravel that wind their way
Among the apple trees and pear trees
Whose shadows are shade.
I come upon an orange lily,
Growing wild against a background of green,
Tall, upright, proud.
My thoughts travel to Belfast,
To the celebrations of this day.
I think of the bands,
The speeches, the flags,
The smoldering ashes
Of last night's bonfires,
The smoldering hate which cannot
Be gathered into garbage vans.
In this Franciscan garden,
So often sanctuary of the persecuted,
The orange and green
Grow side by side.
We learn to live together.

Ruby Tuesday

Moving in the shadows
You spun your web
Of deceit for
The healing of a
Hurt humanity.

Exercising craft with compassion,
You sought to exorcise the demons
Of duplicity,
To clone conscience and
Cause.

To the Protestant a patriot,
To the Catholic,
A provocateur,
You underestimated
The history of their fears,
Their fear of history.

In the end
You lost your cover.
Others lost their lives.

You lost your dream.

Inch Island Presbyterian Church

Visiting the Faithful

Almost two centuries old,
Constructed before the causeway,
The church on Inch Island
Is a short drive from Fahan
Where we walked on the beach,
Listening to Atlantic waves
Wash ashore.

A tractor sits beside the stone wall.
An old man cuts the grass,
Two others weed among the tombstones.
It is 28 years since I preached here
In the days when I thought I was called.

The old man asks my name and gets the keys.
He tells us they're struggling,
Services just twice a month,
Only twenty members,
More pews than people.

I have no survival sermon.
We say a prayer and
Wish him well.

Céide Fields

Damp chills to the bone
As the turfcutter's blade cuts deep
Into ancient fields of undecayed
Heather and purple moor grass,
Peeling back layers of time,
Unearthing Stone Age stone-walled fields
Farmed until Atlantic rains fueled
This blanket of bogland,
Killing the plough,
Preserving the past.

Giant's Causeway

High above columnar basalt cliffs
A white gull begins its swoop
To islands of rock far below,
Wave-cut platforms that rise
Like silent submarines
Patrolling an inhospitable coast
Where moments of stillness are
Shattered by the thunderous crash
Of white angry froth as it washes
The rocks with salt spray.

Set in this amphitheater of glacial
And marine-hewn cliffs, the causeway is
More than a collection of odd-shaped stones,
Cracks and columns, hexagons and pentagons.
Rocky shores and cliff-bound bays abound
With bramble and blackthorn, buttercup and bluebell,
The yellow of flag iris and wind-pruned whin.
Purple heather and thistle look across
The narrow sea to mother Scotland.

The song of stonechat and wren compete with
The call of the curlew and the raucous
Chorus of fulmer and other gulls
Nestling on causeway cliff-tops. At the tideline,
The healthy smell of rotting kelp, once dried,
Will provide the salty taste of dulse.

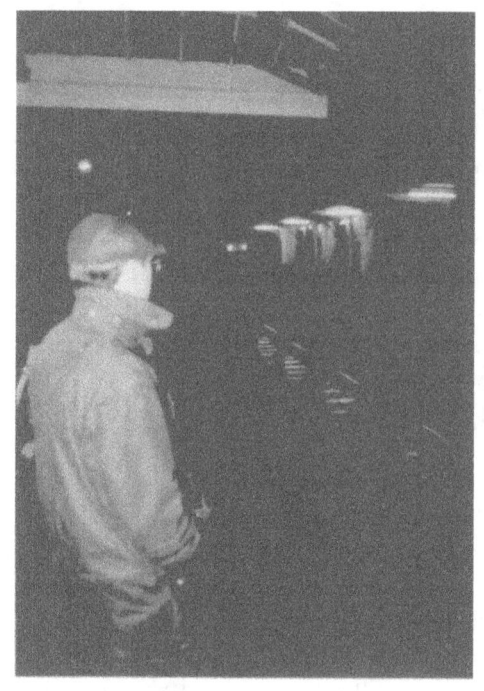

Lisburn Railway Station

Lisburn Railway Station

Ten o'clock,
On a cold October night
I shelter against the station wall.
I look at my watch.
Five minutes.

Above, a light changes from red to green.
In the distance a muffled roar.
My hopes soar,
But the train does not stop.
It rushes through,
Unaware of my disappointment,
Oblivious to my discomfort.

I pace the platform,
Killing time,
Seeking warmth.

Someone flicks a cigarette
Onto the cold concrete.
For a second it glows,
Then fades.

Seconds like minutes,
Minutes like hours,
Nothing to do but wait.

The Shepherd

Directing his collies with whistles and shouts,
The shepherd's sharp voice carries up the slope
To the deserted Slievemore village where we sit
Looking out on blue Atlantic waters
And far-off Clare Island.

He moves the flock through the village ruins
And up the mountain with practiced ease,
His stubbled face ruddy and blistered
From wind and sun.
Twenty years after immigrating to England,
He has returned to Achill Island,
To the peaceful mountains his grandfather
Once crossed to work for a turnip a day
In the famine years.

No one knows how many lived in the village.
Genealogy died with the famine.

Today, grave slabs glisten
As the afternoon sun finds quartz fragments.
The shepherd begins his descent, watching
The unsteady gait of a two-day old lamb
As it tries to keep pace with its mother.

Among tombs of the dead, new life begins.

The Greening of America

Skeletal shadows haunt hillsides silent of song.
Sunken eyes stare sightless across famine fields.
Stinking potatoes permeate the odor of death.

The flux of bloody fever flows from tumbled cottages
Like the tide of ragged remnants flooding the roadside,
Abandoning ditch-dead without ritual or wake.

The human freight of coffin ships sail west
To where the fungus forged its first black root.

SECTION II

The Land of My Exile

Genesis

Now this is the record of the birth of the butterfly.

When its time had come, the humble caterpillar
Attached itself to a twig and after shedding its skin
Withdrew into the dark shell of the chrysalis.

Now there were, at that time, farmers living on the land
And they murmured against the caterpillar, saying,
They are nothing but crop-eating parasites.

But an angel of the Lord appeared unto the caterpillar.
Be not afraid, although you are but larva,
You will be transfigured and become a symbol of the soul.

And so it was,
When the metamorphosis was complete,
A shimmering beauty emerged, delicate and full of grace.

And the butterfly prospered and multiplied,
Painted ladies, wood nymphs, red admirals.
Buttercup yellow, pigmy blue, spring azure.

And the Lord saw that it was good.

MISS MARY McILWAIN
Died May 24th, 1914, after a short illness, Mary, dearly beloved daughter of James and Emily McIlwain, Ligoniel, Belfast Ireland, and niece of Mrs. James L. Ballie Victoria Farm. Newmarket, Ont. The pall bearers were her three uncles Messrs William and Thomas Blain, Mr. James Lyle Ba lie, Mr James Netterfield, Toronto Rev. H. F. Thomas conducted the service at the home and grave Interment in Newmarket Cemetery May 26th.
In a far and distant grave yard
Where the trees t eir branches wave.
Lies a loving niece and daughter
In a cold and silentg rave.
　　　　　Aunt Martha.

Newmarket Cemetery and Obituary

The Photograph

From an envelope in her handbag,
She removed, with care,
The browned black and white
She had preserved for over fifty years.
She remembered the day her sister left,
How she clung to her mother's skirts.
She remembered the day the photograph arrived,
The tears as they gazed at the simple grave,
The handwritten inscription,
    Newmarket, Ontario.

It was the summer of 1976,
Mum's first visit to Canada.
The next Saturday,
As we set out on our search,
Mum told me about Mary.
She was seventeen
When she immigrated to the New World.
Sent to work in a sanitarium,
She contracted tuberculosis and
    Died, age twenty-one.

At the third and oldest cemetery,
The elderly keeper of graves brought us inside his small office.
As he opened the register of the dead,
We watched anxiously until
His unsteady finger stopped at
    McIlwain, Mary.

The old man led us in silence to the grave.
Mum placed fresh flowers by the headstone.
We took new photographs in color, but
As we left the cemetery,
She carefully placed the old black and white
In her purse, an unwritten epitaph,
    Gone but not forgotten.

The View

The mid-afternoon Sunday sun puts winter on hold,
Softening the sensation of cold, casting long-limbed shadows
Across a wooded lot, framed in my attic window.
The wind bends bare branches back and forth,
Back and forth,
Swaying,
Hypnotizing,
But below,
Hibernation on hiatus,
A nimble-footed,
Bushy-tailed scavenger darts across the dead wood,
Foraging for food among the fallen foliage,
Running, jumping, ascending, descending, disappearing,
As I watch the branches sway back and forth,
Back and forth.

Robert Remembered

I have attended quite a few poetry-related events over the years. As best my memory serves me, they all have been free, not too well attended and, for the most part, the poet has been more alive than dead. So it was quite a novelty for me recently to attend a poetry function, on a Saturday night in downtown Knoxville, where the poet was dead—and, along with 300 others, I had to pay $30 for the privilege.

The occasion was Burns Supper—an event celebrated worldwide each January to mark the birth of the Scottish poet Robert Burns. Whether the Supper is celebrated by a faithful few in a private home or by many in a more spacious location, such as The Foundry in Knoxville, the evening is one of much merriment, something the sometimes-bawdy bard would have applauded. It is an evening marked by tradition—the Piper's Call to Supper; saying of Robert Burns *Selkirk Grace;* the Piping in of the Haggis; the Address to the Immortal Memory of Robert Burns, and the reading of a few of Burn's poems.

Of course, the odd skeptic may attribute the large turnout more to the toasting than the poetry, to nationalistic pride rather than literary appreciation or to simple awe of the bard's sexual self-indulgence. However, as Rosemary Rankin-Fraser noted in her Address, it is a measure of the man that, while indeed he loved much, he remains much loved for his gift of words in letter, poem and song; for what he said and how he said it. While the literature of Burns confides infidelity and weakness, paradoxically it conveys honesty and sincerity; his great understanding of human nature; his love of country and strong identification with the language and culture of his day.

It is this heritage that is at the heart of the Knoxville Burns night celebration. Most of the people who attend are of Scots descent. The supper, organized by the Knoxville Scottish Society, provides opportunity for other friends and acquaintances to experience the pageantry of Scotland, including the wearing of national clan attire. The local Chapter, which has approximately 450 members, initiated the Supper in the early 1990s in conjunction with neighboring Maryville College, a Presbyterian College with the motto "The Fighting Scots."

Robert Burns was born in a two-roomed thatched cottage in Alloway, Ayrshire in January 1759. He was the first of seven children born to William Burnes and Agnes Broun.

> Our monarch's hindmost year but ane
> Was five and twenty days begun,
> 'Twas then a blast o' Janwar' Win'
> Blew hansel in on Robin.
> *There was a lad was born in Kyle*

Burnes, a struggling farmer, was a strict Calvinist with a strong work ethic. He put Robert to the plough at an early age and, throughout his life, Burns too maintained this strong work ethos. At one time, he toiled as both Excise Officer and farmer in an attempt to provide for his family. A failure as a farmer, he eventually surrendered the sickle and plough for the pen and the security of a job in local government. But Burns did not adopt his father's Calvinistic convictions. In particular, he disagreed with the doctrine of predestination. Although not written about his father, Burn's poem, *Holy Willie's Prayer*, illustrates his independent thought, firmness of conviction and penchant for humor and satire.

> O thou that in the heavens does dwell!
> Wha, as it pleases best thyself,
> Sends ane to heaven and ten to h-ll,
>   A' for thy glory!
> And no for ony gude or ill
>   They've done before thee.

But more than anything else it was Burn's frequent moral lapses that put him at odds with his father, an issue that remained unresolved at the time of William's death in 1784. Burns fathered at least seven children out of wedlock. Not only did this embarrass his father, but Burns, in a poor attempt at responsibility, left most of the children in the care of his mother, adding to the family financial burden.

Notwithstanding this strained relationship, the poet owed much to his father for ensuring that he received the best education available. But it was his mother and her relatives who first introduced Burns to the Ayrshire folklore that he transformed into verse. With his uncanny ability to marry melody and words, he became a prolific songwriter in the latter part of his life. The third volume of *Scots Musical Museum*, published by James Johnson in 1790, included more than fifty of Burn's songs.

In the Scotland of Burns's time more than half the people spoke Gaelic and few of them understood English. But Burns was from lowland Scotland where the English language was more common. Therefore, his writing frequently was a fusion of Gaelic and English and may be difficult for the reader to comprehend. James Montgomery, another Scot, went so far as to assert that "there is not a poem of Burns composed in a dialect spoken by any class of man in our whole island." However, it says much for the quality of his work that most of us are familiar with Burns's poems and songs without necessarily recognizing Burns as the author. These include, for example, the lines:

The best laid schemes o'mice an' man
To a mouse, on turning her up in her nest, with
The plough

The sweetest hours that e'er I spend
Are spent among the lassies, O
Green Grow the Rashes

Some have meat and cannot eat,
Some can not eat that want it:

But we have meat and we can eat,
Sae let the Lord be thankit.
  Selkirk Grace

Burn's first book of poetry, *Poem's, Chiefly in the Scottish Dialect*, was published in July 1786. Its instant success made Burns a celebrity. This, together with his great personal charm and outstanding gift for conversation, made Burns's services much in demand, both as socialite and lover. The first edition sold out quickly and a second edition was fully subscribed before the printing was complete. It was this revised edition that first included the poem *To a Haggis*. The Haggis, the entrails of a sheep cooked in the sheep's stomach with oatmeal and onions, is served at every Burns Night Supper. Immediately prior to supper, the Haggis is brought in with great ceremony. Accompanied by the scurling sound of Scottish bagpipes, a kilted honor guard escorts the Haggis to the head table and Burns's poem is read in a formal Address to the Haggis. Not all present partake of this delicacy!

The year 1786 also was notable in another respect. In September, Jean Armour, the daughter of a much-respected mason, bore him the first of two sets of twins. Burns had first met Jean two years earlier when she was seventeen. His reputation was such that her parents were outraged by their courtship. When Jean became pregnant, they moved her away. But separation, unfaithfulness and periodic putdowns did not assuage her love for Burns. They eventually married in 1788 and, in spite of his continuing affairs, the marriage lasted until his death in 1796. Ironically, Jean gave birth to their ninth child the day Burns died.

Burns's numerous relationships inspired some of the most tender poems and best-known love songs ever written.

O my Luve's like a red, red rose,
That's newly sprung in June;
O my Luv's like the melodie
That's sweetly play'd in tune.
As fair art thou, my bonie lass,
So deep in luve am I;

And I will luve thee still, my dear,
Till a' the seas gang dry.
O my luve's like a red, red rose

Many of Burns's poems also reflect his agrarian roots and his strong identification with, and empathy for, the simple rustic life. It was such a poem that first brought Burns to the attention of the broader public and while some of the stanzas have been ridiculed as "absurd," others have been used to illustrate the magnificence of his work.

The toil-worn Cotter frae his labor goes,--
This night his weekly moil is at an end,
Collects his spades, his mattocks, and his hoes,
Hoping the morn in ease and rest to spend,
And weary, o'er the moor, his course
   does hameward bend.
The Cotter's Saturday Night

Perhaps the best known of Burns's verse is a song that is sung not only at the conclusion of every Burns Supper, but a song that has become the National Anthem of the New Year:

Should auld acquaintance be forgot,
And never brought to mind?
Should auld acquaintance be forgot,
And auld lang syne!

For auld lang syne, my dear,
   For auld lang syne,
We'll tak a cup of kindess yet,
   For auld lang syne
Auld Lang Syne

Some of Burns's earliest biographers portray him as a drunk whose excesses killed him. However, others point out that Burns liked to present himself as an uneducated peasant. They argue that just as this representation is patently false, so too, his portrayal of himself as a habitual drunkard is seriously exaggerated. More recent scholars attribute his failing health and ultimate death to endocarditis, a heart ailment caused by the heavy labor of his formative years and worsened by harsh winters and a lifelong drive to feel financially secure. In the final analysis, it is the frankness of his writing that makes Burns his own best biographer.

Whatever the reason people go to Burns Supper—fellowship, food, a drop of the barley juice or genuine appreciation of this national hero—few leave unmoved by the tributes to and works of the Immortal Bard. For some, it is the return to hallowed ground. For others, it is the beginning of a journey of exploration. For many, it is the beginning of yet another love affair.

Discord

Words in anger
Make it difficult
To conquer the Everest
Of our differences.

A loose word
Becomes an avalanche,
We return to base in
A wall of silence.

In the desert
We wait for
The other to
Climb down.

Walking with Ophelia

It is the moon of the changing seasons.

Light rain disturbs the innocence of early snow,
Dances delicately on the river below.
A warm breeze dissipates traces of morning fog.
Dying leaves flutter and fall.

The forest is a fiesta of color.

Red dogwood and blue-black sassafras berries
Border the acorn-covered trail.
White oak leaves turn crimson; mulberry leaves yellow.
The maple is a mosaic of scarlet, orange, yellow and red.

The sun is setting for Ophelia.

She establishes her own pace, picks her steps with care.
Nurtured senses are her guide,
Wisdom her walking stick,
Knowledge and nature her companions.

Ophelia is observant.

She points to a smokeless stacked stone chimney,
Traces the hillside slide of a lightning-charred stump,
Spots a solitary vulture ride thermal currents,
Examines the delicate beauty of white wood aster.

Ophelia is a teacher.

She relates the history of old logging camps,
Families digging out coal for subsistence,
The adventures of Daniel Boone,
The rock shelter homes of the Shawnee.

Ophelia shows no fear.

As the trail narrows and steepens,
She hangs on to a cable,
Edges around a large tilting boulder,
Climbs stone steps and switchbacks.

Ophelia is a student.

She rests on the unprotected overlook,
Studies the deep gorge below,
Plays with a large hemlock cone,
Prepares for the downhill hike.

It is now the fall of day.

Ophelia lingers towards the rear,
Talk muted by tired limbs.
In the dusk of owl's light
She tunes her ears to the night.

Born Again

It was not so much
The work of the Divine,
Nor adolescent ascent
To a state of grace,
But the first flush
Of spiritual awakening
That caused my son
To call me a sinner.

I would have repented
Then and there,
But the sight of
My daughter,
Convulsed on the carpet
In theistic titillation,
Caused me too
To lose my composure.

The Drop

We both answer the phone.

Asks a cold male voice,

You paged?

You give him your name,
Ask if he remembers you,
But his few words
Become a hesitant silence,
So you give him another,
Make reference to money
And he leaves to check.

I try to breathe quietly,
My stomach muscles tense.
I know what is coming.

What do you need?

Do you have a bag,
Twenty dollars worth?

OK. Where will you be?

The Underground.

OK.

I put the phone down gently.

By Your Own Hand

You sought death again,
But life won't let go,
So you lie on your back,
Arms straight by your side,
Wrists restrained to the bed,
Head tossing side to side,
Lips parched and black,
Murmuring.

Your body twitches,
You open your eyes,
I touch your tangled hair,
Take your hand,
Try to tell you it's OK,
But you drift away,
Your words, unfathomable
Fragments of fantasy.

Impoetence

Seven months since last
I penned poems of love
To you and
For you.
Because of you
Inspiration came
Unsought
And went away
Again
Unbidden.

Thanksgiving

Harvest,
Another
Gathering.

Kinsfolk
In
Intimate
Visitation.

Bountiful
November
Gratitude.

Love Song

A backdrop of slow, deep drumbeats,
The haunting melody of a stringed orchestra,
The emotive language of lost love
Captured in the flight of a solo oboe,
The slowly building tempo rising for
One last full-throated finale.

Big Creek Trail

The old Indian trail passes
Above the wooded bottoms,
Ascending steadily, but gently,
Along the length of Big Creek.
The soft drop of spring streams,
Seeping from moss-laden bluffs,
Competes with the creek's constant roar
As the waters cascade over gray rocks
And pour into deep green pools
Where shadows of trout reflect
On submerged stone.

Early Retirement

He wanted to talk,
To translate his
Turmoiled thought
So much,
That he sought
Me out.

He tried to be brave,
To save face, but
The tremor of his lips,
A hacking cough
Not present before,
Conveyed the pain.

With tears
In his eyes,
He told me
They had let him go
After twenty years,
And

I sat silent,
Words of solace
Suspended
By his
Shattered
Self-esteem.

On the Run

The flight of the pursued
Had its dawn one summer evening when,
Filled with fantasies of freedom,
She scaled the seven-foot, barbed-wire
Prison fence.

Now, sitting silently by a lake,
On the north shore of Superior,
Far from Fond du Lac and Taycheedah,
Laurie watches the fall moon
With intensity.

She loves to study the night sky,
The Northern Lights. It is like a dream.
She sits as long as she wants to.
No one tells her when to leave.
Time is her prisoner.

Tomorrow, she may ride a bus, go for a walk,
Pick the reddest wood lily, eat an apple
Chosen by herself. But tonight,
She will savor the touch of her young lover.
For ten years she has slept alone.

This freedom is fraught with foreboding.
Laurie is frightened to go out on her own.
She wrestles with choices and decisions.
Apprehensive of apprehension, she watches
What she says and who she talks to.

Soon, before boughs of spruce and silver birch
Weigh heavy with winter snows,
The pursuit will end.
Capture will bring release.
The struggle for freedom
Will recommence
In a solitary cell
In Taycheedah.

Tapestry

Settled among pebbled sand dunes,
Listening to waves wash ashore,
I frame the sun with words,
I paint pelicans skimming shallow seas,
I watch slender sea oats bend
With the breath of morning,
I watch the birth of an
Amelia Island dawn.

Anglers

Beyond the shade of
Wind-angled parasols
At the ocean's edge,
Where whitecaps surrender
And the crest falls forward
Washing the shore
With sea debris,
A line of anglers,
Ankle-deep in foam,
Cast shrimp-baited hooks
Toward deeper blue waters,
Where whitefish hide and
Sailing boats glide and
Sun-drenched surfers
Ride high tide.

ACKNOWLEDGMENTS

To Linda Parsons Marion for editing the original collection of poems and, as teacher and friend, for restoring my joy of writing.

To Cheri Jorgenson for the original book and cover design and getting me started on a publishing career.

To Alicia Adkins for pulling together this revised edition, and for constantly amazing me with your energy, joy, and craziness.

To my extended family in Ireland, Canada, and the United States for your love, encouragement and input. To Philip Gallagher, in particular, for being my wheelman on the photographic shoots.

Cover photograph, photographs related to the poems *Last Ride* and *Visiting the Faithful*, and the essay photographs in *Fencing Frontiers* were provided by James B. Johnston.

Photographs related to the poems *Gentle Man, Origins*, and *The Photograph* were provided by my sister Anna Johnston and my late brother, Raymond Johnston.

Photograph of Farringdon Gardens used with permission of *The Belfast Telegraph*.

Some of the poems and essays included in the revised edition have been published previously. Grateful acknowledgment is made to the editors:

Exile, Stone Wall Fences, and *The Photograph* were included in "All Around Us: Poems from the Valley," published by Blue Ridge Publishing.

Fencing Frontiers was included in "Outscape: writings on fences and frontiers," published by The Knoxville Writers' Guild.

Last Ride and *Lonely Farm* were published by The Presbyterian Herald.

Louvain, Belgium 1971 was published by The Belfast
Telegraph under the title, "We Learn to Live Together."
Robert Remembered and *Walking with Ophelia were
included in "Breathing the Same Air,"* published by
Celtic Cat Publishing and The Knoxville Writers' Guild.
The poem *The Greening of America* won the 2001 Celtic
Heritage prize in the Terry Semple memorial contest.
The poem *Ann* was written for my wife on the twenty-fifth
anniversary of the death of her dear friend, Ann Owens.

ABOUT THE AUTHOR

James B. Johnston was born in Belfast, Northern Ireland. He was educated at Grosvenor High in Belfast and at Trinity College in Dublin. In 1974, he immigrated to Canada and lived in Brampton, Ontario for three years and on the scenic shores of Lake Superior for seven years. He moved to Sylacauga, Alabama in 1994 and to Knoxville, Tennessee in 1990.

Jim founded Celtic Cat Publishing in 1995 to publish emerging and established writers. Celtic Cat has published works by Bill Landry, Marilyn Kallet, Jeff Daniel Marion, Judy Lockhart DiGregorio, Arthur J. Stewart, KB Ballentine, Laura Still, Frank Jamison, Raymond Johnston, Ken Godwin, Angie Vicars, Tracy Bradshaw, and Kathleen Fearing.

About Celtic Cat Publishing

Celtic Cat Publishing was founded in 1995 to publish emerging and established writers. The following works are available from Celtic Cat Publishing at *www.celticcatpublishing.com*, Amazon.com, and major bookstores.

Regional
Appalachian Tales & Heartland Adventures, Bill Landry

Poetry
Marginal Notes, Frank Jamison
Rough Ascension and Other Poems of Science, Arthur J. Stewart
Bushido: The Virtues of Rei and Makoto, Arthur J. Stewart
Circle, Turtle, Ashes, Arthur J. Stewart
Ebbing & Flowing Springs: New and Selected Poems and Prose (1976-2001), Jeff Daniel Marion
Gathering Stones, KB Ballentine
Fragments of Light, KB Ballentine
Guardians, Laura Still

Humor
My Barbie Was an Amputee, Angie Vicars
Life Among the Lilliputians, Judy Lockhart DiGregorio
Memories of a Loose Woman, Judy Lockhart DiGregorio

Chanukah
One for Each Night: Chanukah Tales and Recipes, Marilyn Kallet

Young Adult
Voyage of Dreams: An Irish Memory, Kathleen E. Fearing

Children
Jack the Healing Cat (English), Marilyn Kallet
Jacques le chat guérisseur (French), Marilyn Kallet
Twins, Tracy Ryder Bradshaw

End of Life
Being Alive, Raymond Johnston